T0014554

'Trust and Don't be Afraid' will be a welcome addition to the Christian family's bookshelf. Beginning with Genesis and working through to Revelation Jean Stapleton traces the experience of fear through 40 carefully chosen Bible stories. Each story is followed by a scripture reading and some questions for children to discuss with their parents or try to answer themselves. The author's choice to stories introduces different kinds of fear: of the future, of hopeless situations, under persecution, of the unexpected, because of disobedience, of a guilty conscience, of making wrong decisions and others. The fear of God that is the beginning of wisdom is woven through the text like a golden thread.

Irene Howat

Award winning author and ghost–writer
for multiple children's books

10 9 8 7 6 5 4 3 2 1

Copyright © 2022 Jean Stapleton

ISBN: 978-1-5271-0895-0

Published by Christian Focus Publications,
Geanies House, Fearn, Tain, Ross-shire,
IV20 1TW, Scotland, U.K.
www.christianfocus.com;
email: info@christianfocus.com

Designed and typeset by Pete Barnsley (CreativeHoot.com)

Printed and bound by Imago, Turkey

Trust
God
and don't be
Afraid

40 BIBLE READINGS ABOUT FAITH

JEAN STAPLETON

CF4·K

Contents

Introduction

Have you ever felt afraid? Small children are often afraid of the dark. Young people may be afraid of not being accepted by others. Adults may have all sorts of fears about the future. It is not surprising then, that in the Bible the words '**fear not**' or '**do not be afraid**' occur quite frequently. The God who made us, knows all about our fears.

In this book, we read of all sorts of situations where people were fearful. Some were told by God not to fear, some were given this message by a prophet. Sometimes the appearance of an angel caused fear, but this was always followed by the encouragement not to be afraid. We also read of people who trusted God and reminded others that they need not fear, because God was with them.

Our own trust in God is strengthened as we learn from the Bible, how the God who helped His people to face difficulties without fear, will also help us if we trust in Him.

Jean Stapleton

1 Courageous Rescue
(Genesis 15:1)

Abraham had acted swiftly to rescue his nephew Lot, who had been taken captive in a battle between local kings. Abraham also brought back other captives, as well as goods that had been stolen. The King of Sodom wanted to give Abraham a reward for his actions. Abraham however refused to take anything from the King of Sodom. Abraham depended on God and would not allow anyone else to claim that they had made him rich.

We do not know how Abraham felt after this, if he felt exhausted or afraid that he might be attacked by the people who lived around him. The Bible does tell us, however, what God said to Abraham: '**Do not be afraid**, Abraham …' God would be his shield and would reward him, for he had fought bravely and had refused any reward from a godless king.

Abraham lived among people who had no knowledge of the true God. Christians today live among people who often claim that they do not even believe that there is a God. What they really mean is that they do not want to think about the God who made them, and who tells them how they ought to behave. Many people simply want to live as they please with no thought of their Creator.

Remember that Abraham's God is still the same today as He was when Abraham lived. He still protects and provides for those who trust in Him.

Read

Genesis chapter 14, and 15:1-6; John 14:1-6, and verse 27; Matthew 28:20.

Questions

1. There is a promise in Matthew 28:20. How will this help a young Christian who has no Christian friends at school?

2. How did Abraham show his dependence on God? (Genesis 14:22-23). What should a Christian not do to gain wealth? – give examples.

2 When Hagar Lost Hope
(Genesis 21:17)

Sarah was seventy-five years old. It was ten years since God had promised Abraham that he would have many descendants and they still had no children. Sarah suggested to Abraham that he should take her maid Hagar to be his second wife. Sarah was sure that if Hagar had a child, that child would be hers.

Hagar gave birth to a son who was named Ishmael. But Sarah's plan did not go as she had expected. First of all, Hagar looked down on her mistress because she had no children of her own. Then Hagar ran away because Sarah had started treating her harshly. Hagar eventually did return, after an angel told her that she must.

At last, when Sarah was ninety years old, she had the son God had promised. He was named Isaac, the name God had given him.

There came a day when Sarah saw Ishmael laughing at her little son. She told Abraham that Hagar and Ishmael must go. Abraham was troubled, but God told him that this must happen. However, God promised that Ishmael's descendants would also become a nation.

Hagar and Ishmael were sent away the next day. Abraham gave them food and water. As they wandered about in the desert, the water was used up. Hagar thought her son would die of thirst. Then she heard an angel saying, '**Fear not.**' God helped her to see that there was a well and she gave Ishmael a drink which revived him.

There are times in life when we lose hope: we cannot see a way out of our troubles. God is able to help us, just as He helped Hagar when no other help was to be found.

Read

Genesis 21:1-21; Psalm 46:1.

Questions

1. What actions of Hagar showed that she had no hope? (Genesis 21:15-16).

2. What words of the angel show us that God is always aware of events? (Genesis 21:17).

3. What does the Psalmist say about the help that God gives? (Psalm 46:1).

3 Trouble About the Water
(Genesis 26:24)

Abraham and Sarah had waited twenty-five years for the birth of the son God had promised them. They named him Isaac, as God had instructed them. When he was forty years old, Isaac married Rebekah, who was the granddaughter of Abraham's brother, Nahor. After they had been married for twenty years, Isaac and Rebekah had twin boys, Esau and Jacob.

After the death of his father, Isaac moved to Gerar, a town on the border of the land of the Philistines. God gave Isaac prosperity and the Philistines became envious of him. They asked him to move away from them and he did so. A good water supply was very important in that hot, dry climate. However, the Philistines had blocked the wells that Abraham's servants had dug. Isaac's servants began clearing them but local herdsmen squabbled over the first two wells that they tried to clear. The third well did not cause trouble though and Isaac and his servants had the water supply they needed. Isaac then moved to Beersheba, about halfway between the Mediterranean Sea and the southern end of the Dead Sea.

God spoke to Isaac at Beersheba. He promised to be with Isaac, and He renewed the promises He had made to Abraham. God said, '**do not fear**, for I am with you ...'

Isaac was surrounded by many people who did not know God, and who were envious of his prosperity. These people were potential enemies. How reassuring to be told that he need not be afraid because God would be with him.

Read

Genesis 26; Hebrews 11:8-20.

Questions

1. What did Abraham and Isaac have that enabled them to believe God's promise? (Hebrews 11:8 and 20).

2. In Hebrews 11 what verses make it clear that both Abraham and Isaac believed that God's promises would be fulfilled?

4 An Old Man's Journey
(Genesis 46:3)

Jacob was one hundred and thirty years old when he left the land of Canaan for Egypt. Why did such an old man set out on a journey to another country? There must have been a special reason, and there was. In Egypt he would see the son who he thought had been killed many years before. Jacob had a special love for Joseph, but Joseph's brothers had convinced him that his son had been killed by a wild animal. The truth of the matter was that they had sold him to slave traders.

The full story of Joseph's life in Egypt is found in Genesis chapters 37 and 39-45. After years of unjust treatment, Joseph became a very important man in Egypt, second only to the Pharaoh. During a time of famine, Joseph's brothers travelled to Egypt to buy food. When Joseph made himself known to them, he told them to bring their families and their father to Egypt, where he would provide for them.

At first, Jacob could not believe the news that Joseph was alive. But once he was convinced that it was true, he willingly set out for Egypt. Stopping at Beersheba in the south of Canaan, Jacob offered sacrifices to

God. That night, God spoke to him in a vision. 'I am God ... **do not fear** to go down to Egypt ... I will go down with you ...'

What comforting words these were for Jacob. God also promised to make a great nation from Jacob's family, while they lived in Egypt.

If we have trusted in the Lord Jesus Christ as our Saviour, we also have His promise that He will never leave us. Whether it is a new school, a new job, a new home or a new land, we will not go alone.

Read

Genesis 45:17-28 and 46:1-7.

Questions

1. Did Joseph blame or punish his brothers for the way they had treated him? Why did he act as he did? (Genesis 45:4-8).

2. How did Jacob react to the news that Joseph was alive? (Genesis 45:25-28).

5 Ten Frightened Men
(Genesis 50:19-20)

Joseph was an important man in Egypt: only the Pharaoh was greater than he was. However, Egypt was not Joseph's home country. Until he was seventeen years old, he had lived in the land of Canaan. He was the eleventh son of Jacob, Abraham's grandson. He had one younger brother whose name was Benjamin.

As a young man Joseph's ten older brothers hated him because their father had a special love for him. They sold him to traders who took him to Egypt and sold him as a slave. Joseph's life is told in the Book of Genesis. He was a slave, imprisoned for a crime he did not commit, but then became Pharaoh's second in command.

When famine arrived Joseph's brothers came to Egypt to buy grain. They met Joseph but did not recognise him. When he made himself known to them, they were afraid that they would be punished for their treatment of him. Joseph however was kind and told them to bring their father and their families to Egypt. He would look after them while the famine continued. Seventeen years passed, then Jacob died at the great age of 147. Once again the ten brothers became afraid: they still carried the guilt of what they had done so long ago. Maybe now, they thought, Joseph would make them suffer for what they had done.

Joseph again told his brothers not to be afraid. Joseph believed that although his brothers had wanted to harm him, God had provided a way for the whole family to be cared for during the seven long years of famine.

If you have ever had a guilty conscience about something you have done, you will understand how Joseph's brothers felt. The Lord Jesus is able to free us from our guilt. He died on the cross to suffer the punishment for the sin of everyone who trusts in Him.

Read

Genesis 45:1-13; 50:14-21; Romans 8:28.

Questions

1. Why were Joseph's brothers afraid?

2. What helped Joseph to forgive his brothers? (Genesis 45:5-8).

3. How do we see the truth of Romans 8:28 working out in Joseph's life?

6 When Many People Were Afraid

(Exodus 14:13)

The Israelites had left their life of slavery in Egypt behind. They were on a journey to the land God had promised to the descendants of Abraham. God gave Moses directions for the beginning of the journey. They must go towards the Red Sea and make their camp near there. But the people saw something that made them very afraid.

Pharaoh had second thoughts about letting the Israelites go. He led his army in pursuit. This was what the Israelites saw. They found themselves trapped between the Egyptian army and its chariots and the Red Sea. The Israelites called on God for help, but they also complained to Moses that it would have been better for them to stay in Egypt.

It seemed to be a hopeless situation, Moses spoke to the people, '**Do not be afraid**.' Moses was calm because God had told him what was going to happen. He had also told him that God would gain the victory over Pharaoh and his army. Moses believed God and was unafraid.

We read in Exodus chapter 14 how God made a path through the sea, so that the Israelites went across on dry ground. When the Egyptians followed them, they were all drowned. Pharaoh was proud and had refused to obey God. Too late he learned that, unlike his useless idols, Israel's God was a great and powerful God.

Becoming a Christian does not mean that we will never face any difficulties. It is good to remember that the God we trust in can bring us through all sorts of difficult times, as He did for His people in Old Testament days.

Read

Exodus chapter 14; Psalm 27:1-3.

Questions

1. Describe the frightening situation that the Israelites were in.

2. What made the difference between Moses' reaction and the people's fear?

3. What gave the Psalmist confidence even in a time of war? (Psalm 27:1-3).

7 God Speaks to the People
(Exodus 20:20)

The Israelites' journey brought them to the wilderness of Sinai and they camped near Mount Sinai. They stayed in this area for about a year, because God had much to teach them before they entered their own land. First, God gave them His 'rules for life': the Ten Commandments.

Moses gave the people instructions, that on a particular day, they must not go on to Mount Sinai or touch it. They stood at the foot of the mountain and saw lightning and a thick cloud on it. The mountain smoked and quaked and the people trembled, as they saw something of the power of God. Then God spoke the words of the Ten Commandments.

The people were very afraid. So powerful was God's presence that they feared they would die if God continued speaking to them in that way. They pleaded with Moses that God would not speak directly to them again. Moses said, '**Do not fear**; for God has come to test you, and that His fear may be before you, so that you may not sin.'

Moses was able to tell the people not to fear, because he knew that God was teaching the people that their God had spoken to them from heaven. They must not make idols like the nations around them. The true God had spoken: they had heard His voice and seen something of His power.

We read in the New Testament that we do not come to God in a way that makes us afraid. We come through our Mediator – the Lord Jesus, who died so that our sin can be forgiven. God's commandments show us how sinful we are, so that we understand why we need a Saviour.

Read

Exodus chapters 19 and 20; Hebrews 12:18-24.

Questions

1. What promise did the people make? (Exodus 19:5-8).

2. Why were the people afraid? (Exodus 20:18-19).

3. What did God say that the people must not do? (Exodus 20:23).

8 When Fear Led to Disobedience
(Numbers 14:9)

The Israelites were close to the land God had promised them. Twelve men, one from each tribe of Israel, had travelled to the land of Canaan and brought back a report to Moses and the people. The report was good: the land was fertile, good for growing crops. The twelve spies brought some of the fruit: grapes, figs and pomegranates. But there was a problem.

Ten of the spies said that the people of Canaan were strong and lived in well-fortified cities. Their advice was that the Israelites were not strong enough to take over the land. Just two spies, Joshua and Caleb, spoke differently. They said, '… do not rebel against the Lord, nor fear the people of the land … the Lord is with us. **Do not fear** them.'

Sadly, the people were greatly afraid. They began complaining to Moses and Aaron. They threatened to choose another leader and return to Egypt. Joshua and Caleb were not able to calm them down.

The people of Israel should have trusted in God because they had seen God's power displayed when they crossed the Red Sea. Moses pleaded with God not to destroy the people, even though that was what they deserved. God said He would forgive them, but He would not give the land to those who had disobeyed Him. The Israelites would wander in the wilderness for forty years. All those over twenty years old, except Joshua and Caleb, would die in the wilderness. It would be their children who would one day live in Canaan.

Unbelief leads to disobedience. The people of Israel were afraid because they did not believe that God would help them. They disobeyed God's instruction to enter Canaan. Faith leads to obedience as you will see when you read Hebrews 11.

Read

Numbers 13:1-3 and 17-33; 14:1-9; Hebrews 11.

Questions

1. What did all twelve spies agree about? (Numbers 13:27).

2. What was different about Joshua and Caleb's report? (Numbers 13:30-31).

3. Why should the Israelites have known that God would help them? (Exodus 14:21-22).

9 The New Leader
(Joshua 1:9)

Joshua had been given an enormous task. For forty years, Moses had led the Israelites. Now Moses was dead and God had chosen Joshua to lead the people of Israel into the land of Canaan. Joshua was known to the people as a courageous and faithful man. He had led them against an enemy who attacked them after they had left Egypt (Exodus 17:9-13). Then with Caleb, he had encouraged the people of Israel to go into the land of Canaan. At that time the people refused to obey God and so had spent forty years in the wilderness during which Joshua had also been Moses' assistant.

Now the heavy responsibility of leading God's people was his. In the first chapter of the Book of Joshua, we have God's words of encouragement to Joshua, '... **do not be afraid**, nor be dismayed, for the Lord your God is with you wherever you go.'

It is not difficult to understand why Joshua could have been fearful and dismayed at the task before him. At this time, the Israelites probably numbered at least two million people. The land they were to enter was already inhabited. God had given the Canaanites many years to repent of their evil ways, but they had not done so. The Israelites were instructed to destroy these people and then divide the land between their twelve tribes.

Joshua trusted God's promise and he did carry out the task that God had given him. He is an example of how faith leads to obedience.

Read

Joshua 1:1-11 and chapter 3; John 14:15.

Questions

1. Why was Joshua not to be afraid? (Joshua 1:9).

2. How do we know that Joshua had faith in God's promises? (Joshua 1:1-2 and chapter 3).

3. How do we show that we love the Lord Jesus and have faith in Him? (John 14:15).

10 An Unexpected Defeat
(Joshua 8:1)

After a great victory at Jericho, Joshua had not expected defeat at the next city, Ai. God explained the reason for Israel's defeat. Someone had disobeyed God's instruction that the people must not take anything from Jericho for themselves. The sinner must be identified and the sin punished.

Joshua followed God's instructions. He went through the tribes, then the families, until he came to one man, Achan. Achan confessed that he had taken gold, silver and clothing from Jericho. He had hidden these in his tent. Achan was put to death: his sin had caused Israel's defeat.

It was not easy to attack Ai a second time. The people of that city would have been confident that they could win again. God spoke to Joshua: '**Do not be afraid** … See, I have given into your hand the king of Ai, his people, his city, and his land.' Strengthened by God's words, Joshua led the Israelites to victory once again.

There are lessons for us to learn from the events at Ai. All Christians have battles to fight, and God has provided armour for us (Ephesians 6:10-18). We will all, at some time, know temptation from the devil. He is the enemy of all those who love God. We also have our own particular weak points. Some of us are quick-tempered, others are prone to speak too quickly and thoughtlessly, some are envious of other people's success or possessions.

When we give way to sinful words or actions, we know that God will forgive us if we confess our sin to Him (1 John 1:9). But we may feel defeated and like Joshua, need God's word of encouragement.

Read

Joshua chapters 7 and 8:1-3; Isaiah 41:10; Ephesians 6:10-18.

Questions

1. Why were the Israelites defeated at Ai? (Joshua 7:11).

2. Describe the steps to disobedience that Achan took. (Joshua 7:21).

3. Memorise Isaiah 41:10.

11 When Five Kings Attacked
(Joshua 10:8)

Some people from the city of Gibeon had deceived the Israelites. They had pretended that they were from a far country and they made a peace agreement with Israel. A few days later it was discovered that the Gibeonites lived in Canaan, not in some distant land. The Israelites should have taken over their land, but the leaders said they must keep to the agreement they had made.

Adoni-Zedek was the king of Jerusalem. He had heard how Jericho and Ai had been taken by Israel. He also heard that the Gibeonites had made peace with Israel. He persuaded four other local kings to join him in attacking Gibeon.

Men from Gibeon came to Joshua for help. Joshua led his army to help the people of Gibeon. It was no small thing to go against five kings, but God spoke to Joshua, '**Do not fear** them, for I have delivered them into your hand ...'

Joshua led a surprise attack on the enemy and many were killed. Others fled, but God sent large hailstones that killed more men than the battle had done. Joshua then called on God to lengthen the day by not allowing the sun to set at its normal time. This request shows Joshua's faith: only the God who created the sun could possibly do such a thing. God granted Joshua's request and Israel was able to complete the defeat of the five kings, who were all killed even though they had tried to hide in a cave.

The people who lived in Canaan worshipped idols and lived very wicked lives. God had given them many years to change their ways, but they had not done so. God still allows people time to repent of their sin, but where there is no repentance, God will punish sin. The good news is that the Lord Jesus has taken sin's punishment for all who repent and trust in Him.

Read

Joshua 9:1-19; 10:1-15; 2 Peter 3:9.

Questions

1. What did the leaders fail to do? (Joshua 9:14).

2. What was the miracle that God performed in answer to Joshua's request? (Joshua 10:12-14).

3. Why does God not always punish wrongdoers quickly? (2 Peter 3:9).

12 When Gideon Feared the Angel of the LORD

(Judges 6:23)

The Israelites settled in the land of Canaan. After the death of Joshua, there were times when they turned to the false gods of the Canaanites. When this happened, God allowed enemies to overcome them until they realised that they needed His help. When the people called on God to help them, He gave them men called Judges, to lead them.

For seven years the Israelites were troubled by people called Midianites, who destroyed their crops and animals. When the people called on God to help them, He sent a prophet to them. The prophet explained that their trouble was because they had disobeyed God.

After this, the Angel of the LORD came and spoke to Gideon. He told Gideon that he must save the Israelites from the Midianites. Gideon could not understand how he could do this, but God promised to be with him.

When we read of the Angel of the LORD in the Old Testament, we know that this was the Son of God appearing as an angel. When Gideon realised who it was who had spoken to him and received an offering from him, he was afraid. Then God spoke to him, 'Peace be with you; **do not fear**, you shall not die.'

The Bible tells us that there is a right fear of God. This does not mean being frightened. It does mean having respect (reverence) for God, because He is so much greater than we are. In Old Testament times, the High Priest was the only person who could enter the Most Holy Place in the Tabernacle. Even he could only go in once a year and then only after he had made an offering for his own sin, and the sin of the people. If we have trusted in the Lord Jesus to forgive our sin, we can know God as our Friend and speak to Him anywhere. But we always speak to God with reverence, because He is the great Creator and He is holy.

Read Judges 6:1-23.

Questions

1. Why were the Israelites in trouble? (verses 7-10).

2. What was to be Gideon's task, and did he feel able to do this? (verses 14-15).

3. What encouragement did Gideon receive? (verses 14 and 16).

13 Kind Words for Ruth
(Ruth 3:11)

Ruth was a Moabite widow living in a strange land. She had married a son of Elimelech and Naomi, who had moved from Israel to Moab in a time of famine. But Elimelech and Ruth's husband Mahlon had both died, as well as Mahlon's brother Chilion, who had married Orpah. Naomi decided to return to Israel where the famine was over. Ruth had come to trust in the true God, and she was determined to stay with her mother-in-law.

Back in Naomi's hometown of Bethlehem, the two women were poor. They had no-one to support them and life for a widow was difficult. Ruth willingly went to the fields to glean. Gleaning was God's provision for the poor. The people of Israel were instructed to leave crops in the corners of their fields as well as anything the reapers dropped, for those who were so poor that they were in need of their daily food.

To Naomi's great joy, Ruth had gleaned in the field of a man named Boaz. Boaz was a wealthy relation of Elimelech, and he was kind to Ruth, having heard of her kindness to Naomi. It was a law of God, that a near relation could buy back the possessions of a man who had died, and also marry his widow. Naomi knew this and she told Ruth what she must do. This involved a visit to a place where threshing was done at the end of the barley harvest.

Ruth carried out her mother-in-law's instructions and Boaz understood what was required of him. He spoke kindly to Ruth, '… **do not fear**, I will do for you all that you request …' After giving a closer relative the opportunity to act as 'Kinsman Redeemer', Boaz did buy back Mahlon's possessions and also married Ruth. (A kinsman is a relative, and a redeemer is someone who buys something back.) Ruth and Naomi were no longer poor and when Naomi nursed her little grandson, Obed, she found great happiness after her years of sadness.

Read The book of Ruth.

Questions

1. Who is our Redeemer and what did He give for our Redemption? (1 Peter 1:18-19).

2. Who was Ruth's great-grandson and who else came from his family? (Matthew 1:5-6 and verse 16).

14 When the People were Afraid Because they had Sinned
(1 Samuel 12: 20)

Samuel had been Israel's chosen leader for many years. He had travelled on a circuit between three cities, Bethel, Gilgal and Mizpah, then returning to his home in Ramah. In each of these places he judged the cases that were brought to him, solving the problems that arose between people. He also taught the people to be faithful to God and to obey Him.

There came a time when the people of Israel wanted a king, like the nations around them. From the time of Moses and Joshua, and through all the years of the Judges, God had chosen men to lead His people. Samuel was saddened by the people's request, but God told him to do as they asked. He would show Samuel who their king should be. The man appointed to be Israel's first king was Saul from the tribe of Benjamin.

Saul was introduced to the people as their king and later there was a gathering at Gilgal where this was confirmed. There Samuel spoke to the people of many things that had happened to them. How they had turned to idols and then called on God to keep them when trouble came. How God answered by raising up a leader. All this time, God had been their King.

That day Samuel called on God to send rain and thunder and when God did so, the people became afraid because of all their sins. Samuel spoke again, '**Do not fear** …' He told them that even though they had sinned, they must continue to obey God and not go after useless idols. Samuel assured the people that God would not leave them, because He had made them His people. But they were once again warned that if they stopped obeying God, they would forfeit His blessing.

Read

1 Samuel 8:1–9, and chapter 12.

Questions

1. What was the sin that was repeated in the life of the nation of Israel? (1 Samuel 12:9-10).

2. What was wrong with the request for a king? (1 Samuel 12:12).

3. What promise did Samuel make? (1 Samuel 12:19 and 23).

15 Fear of the King
(2 Samuel 9:7)

Mephibosheth had been sent for by King David. He had reason to be afraid, because his grandfather, King Saul, had tried to have David killed. In fact, David had to move from one place to another because King Saul was constantly searching for him. But there was also a reason why Mephibosheth did not need to be afraid. His father, Jonathan, had been David's greatest friend. David had promised that he would show kindness to Jonathan's family.

It seems that Mephibosheth was fearful as he bowed down before the king. It would not have been unusual for King David to have taken revenge on Saul's descendants. But almost David's first words were reassuring, '**Do not fear**, for I will surely show you kindness for Jonathan your father's sake …'

King David made Mephibosheth understand that he would have all the land that had belonged to King Saul. He would also have servants to manage the land for him. Besides all this, he was to have his meals at the king's table.

Mephibosheth had not done anything to deserve the king's kindness. He was treated kindly because of David's promise to his father, Jonathan. This is like a picture of God's grace to all who trust in the Lord Jesus. Grace means undeserved favour. We are not accepted by God because of our goodness, in fact we are sinful and have no real goodness of our own. God shows us kindness that we do not deserve, when we ask Him to forgive our sin, because the Lord Jesus died to take sin's punishment for us. David showed kindness to Mephibosheth for Jonathan's sake. God shows kindness to us for Jesus' sake.

Read

2 Samuel chapter 9; Ephesians 1:7; John 3:16.

Questions

1. Why did King David show kindness to Mephibosheth? (2 Samuel 9:1).

2. Why does God show kindness to sinful people?

3. Learn the words of John 3:16.

16 A Widow who Feared Starvation
(1 Kings 17:13)

Zarephath was a town on the Mediterranean coast, north of Israel. One day, a widow who lived there with her son, met a stranger. It was a time of famine, and the widow was collecting sticks to cook her very last flour and oil. The stranger was the prophet Elijah. He asked the widow to bring him some water to drink. As she went to bring him a drink, he asked her for some bread.

The poor woman told Elijah that she had no bread. She was just about to cook the flour and oil that was all that she had left. Elijah said, '**Do not fear** …' He told her to make something for him and then for her and her son. He explained that God had promised that her flour and oil would last until He sent rain, and then the crops would grow again.

It would not be easy to give the last food you had to a stranger. But this stranger spoke with the authority of a prophet. The widow showed that she believed what Elijah had said, by doing as he told her. Elijah stayed with the widow and her son, and they had enough food while the famine lasted.

The reason for the famine was that God had not sent rain because of the idolatry of the people. The time of famine should have taught them that their idols were useless and could not help them. Elijah was faithful to God and God provided for him and for the poor widow who helped him.

This true story of Elijah at Zarephath, reminds us that God is able to protect and provide for those who trust in Him. We all meet with trouble or difficulty at some time. God knows our needs and He hears our prayers when we call on Him to help us.

Read

1 Kings 17:1-16; Psalm 23 *(The word 'want' in verse 1 means, not being without anything I need.)*

Questions

1. How was Elijah provided for at the beginning of the famine? (1 Kings 17:3-6).

2. What was the widow afraid of? (1 Kings 17:12-13).

3. Why could Elijah be confident that the widow did not need to be fearful? (1 Kings 17:14).

17 When the Prophet's Servant was Afraid

(2 Kings 6:16)

The king of Syria was troubled. It seemed that one of his servants must be giving information to the king of Israel. Every time he sent men to attack part of Israel, he found someone on guard there. Who among his servants could be warning the enemy of where the next attack would be?

The king spoke to his servants about it. One of them assured him that none of them had done such a thing. He explained that it was Elisha the prophet who was giving the warnings to the king of Israel. When the king of Syria knew that Elisha was in the city of Dothan, he sent a great army with horses and chariots to surround the city. This was done in the night. In the morning, Elisha's servant saw the Syrian army and he was afraid.

Elisha told his servant, '**Do not fear**, for those who are with us are more than those who are with them.' The prophet prayed that God would let his servant see their protectors. Then the servant saw horses and chariots of fire all around Elisha.

Elisha was able to lead the Syrians to the king of Israel. On Elisha's advice, the king of Israel gave the Syrians a good meal and sent them away. After this, the Syrians stopped sending raiders into Israel.

Becoming a Christian does not mean that life will always be easy. Christians in many countries are persecuted just because they are Christians. Even in Europe and America there are people who try to make life difficult for those who trust in the Lord Jesus Christ. We need to remember the true story of Elisha and his servant. We cannot see Jesus now, but we have His promise that He will never leave those who trust in Him (Hebrews 13: 5).

Read

2 Kings 6:8-23; Psalm 34:6-7; Hebrews 13:5.

Questions
1. Why was the king of Syria troubled? (2 Kings 6:11).

2. Why was Elisha's servant afraid? (2 Kings 6:15).

3. Why was Elisha able to tell his servant not to be afraid? (2 Kings 6:16).

18 Words to Produce Fear
(2 Kings 19:6)

Words can be very important in time of war. They can be chosen to produce fear. The King of Assyria sent some of his officers with a great army to Jerusalem. The officers spoke so that the people of Jerusalem heard in their own language about the power of the Assyrians. They were also told not to let their king, Hezekiah, persuade them to trust in God for help. No other nation had been kept safe by their gods.

A report was brought to King Hezekiah. He sent his officials to Isaiah the prophet, to tell him that the Assyrians were speaking against God Himself. Isaiah gave them a message from God for King Hezekiah: '**Do not be afraid** of the words which you have heard, with which the servants of the king of Assyria have blasphemed Me.'

God had also told Isaiah that the King of Assyria would hear something that would cause him to return to his own land.

When the King of Assyria's officers returned to him, they found him fighting against another city in Israel. From there he sent a threatening letter to King Hezekiah. Hezekiah took the letter to the temple and prayed that God would save Jerusalem. God answered Hezekiah's prayer. The people of Judah did not have to fight against the Assyrians. God destroyed many Assyrian soldiers and the king went back to Nineveh, where he was killed by two of his own sons.

King Hezekiah's situation had seemed impossible: the Assyrians were much stronger than the people of Jerusalem. But God dealt with their pride, by His own great power. We should always remember that our God is the great Creator and He is able to act powerfully, at the right time.

Read

2 Kings 18:17-37; 19:1-19 and 32-37.

Questions

1. How did the Assyrians try to frighten the people of Jerusalem? (2 Kings 18:33-35).

2. What did King Hezekiah understand that the Assyrians did not understand? (2 Kings 19:15-19).

19 A Father's Encouragement
(1 Chronicles 22:13)

King David knew that his son Solomon had a very special task to do when he became king. It was a task that he had wanted to do himself: to build a temple at Jerusalem. God had said, 'no' to David, but promised him that the temple would be built when Solomon was king. David had been a man of war, overcoming Israel's enemies. His son's reign would be a time of peace.

David made preparation for the temple, even though he would never see it. He had gold, silver, bronze, iron, wood and precious stones. The Holy Spirit had helped David to understand how the temple should be built, and he gave these plans to his son.

King David knew that his reign was coming to an end. He spoke to Solomon, encouraging him to do the special work that God had given him, and to keep the laws that God had given to Moses.

Solomon was young. Would he be afraid of the responsibility of being the king of Israel, with the added responsibility of making sure that the temple was completed? David spoke words to reassure him,

'Be strong and of good courage; **do not fear** nor be dismayed.' He also spoke to the leaders of the people, that they must help Solomon, '… arise and build the sanctuary of the Lord God …'

David had gone through difficult times, especially when he was pursued by King Saul who wanted him to be killed. He had learned to trust God and not give way to fear. He passed on to his son what he had learned: when God is with you, there is no need to be afraid.

Read

1 Chronicles 22:5-19, and 29:1-19.

Questions

1. Why had God chosen Solomon, not David, to build the temple? (1 Chronicles 22:7-10).

2. How did David show how important the building of the temple was to him? (1 Chronicles 29:2-5).

3. What reasons could Solomon have had for being fearful?

20 When Enemies were Ready to Attack
(2 Chronicles 20:15)

King Jehoshaphat was afraid. He had heard bad news: a very large army was on its way to the kingdom of Judah (the southern part of the land of Israel). Jehoshaphat went into the court of the temple and called upon God. He spoke of how God had promised to hear the prayers of His people from the temple. He admitted that he did not know what to do when faced with the armies of Moab, Ammon, and other nations.

A prophet named Jahaziel brought God's answer to Jehoshaphat's prayer. '**Do not be afraid** nor dismayed because of this great multitude, for the battle is not yours, but God's.' God gave instructions as to what should be done, but He assured the people that they would not need to fight.

The king and the people bowed down and worshipped God. Early the next day, Jehoshaphat encouraged the people to believe their God. He then appointed singers to go ahead of the army, praising God.

The various nations that made up the army approaching Judah, began fighting and killing each other. As

Jehoshaphat and his people came towards their enemies, all they found were dead bodies. They collected a lot of valuables and jewellery which they took back to Judah. They returned to the temple, still praising God.

It always helps us to remember that God does not change. He will still answer the prayers of nations who call upon Him. During the second world war, the King of the United Kingdom called for national days of prayer. History records how those prayers were answered, sometimes in changes in the weather at sea, sometimes in changes to the enemies' plans.

Read

2 Chronicles 20:1-30; 2 Chronicles 7:12-16.

Questions

1. What did Jehoshaphat do when he was afraid? (2 Chronicles 20:6-12).

2. Find the words that reassured the king and his people, in 2 Chronicle 20:15 and 21.

3. What was the promise that God had given to King Solomon, after the building of the temple? (2 Chronicles 7:14 and 15).

21 A Conspiracy Discovered
(Nehemiah 4:14)

Nehemiah was among the Jewish exiles living in Persia. He was 'cupbearer' to King Artaxerxes, which means that he was responsible for the king's wine. When he heard news from Jerusalem, that the walls of the city were broken down and its gates burned, he was very sad. He spent several months praying about this state of affairs. His prayers were answered, as God gave him an opportunity to speak to the king and the king was willing to help.

Nehemiah was allowed to go to Jerusalem, where he supervised the re-building of the city walls. This was not an easy task, as there were men who opposed the work. They even made a secret plan to attack the work. But Nehemiah heard about the conspiracy and he took action. He put armed men in positions to be ready for any attack. He also encouraged the people, '**Do not be afraid** of them. Remember the Lord, great and awesome …'

The Jews' enemies heard that their plans were known and so the attack came to nothing. But Nehemiah kept some of the armed men on guard, while others continued the building. Even the builders had their swords with them.

In spite of the conspiracy and other methods of trying to stop the work, the walls were completed in just fifty-two days. Nehemiah understood something of the greatness and power of the God he trusted in. But he was also a practical man: he prayed and he worked. We need to pray about any difficulties we face. We also need to ask God to help us to take the right action for the situation.

Read

Nehemiah chapter 1; 2:1-6 and chapter 4.

Questions

1. What did Nehemiah do when he heard about the state of Jerusalem? (1:4).

2. What did Nehemiah do when the king asked him what he wanted? (2:4-5).

3. What reason did Nehemiah give to the people, that meant they did not need to be afraid of an attack by their enemies? (4:14).

22 Fear of What Others May Say
(Isaiah 51:7)

Isaiah was chosen by God to be a prophet to the people of Judah. His task was to give God's messages to the people, but he knew that they would not always want to hear. Isaiah was given a great deal to say about the coming of the promised Saviour. For example, in Isaiah chapter 53 we have an explanation and description of the crucifixion of the Lord Jesus, 700 years before it happened. But he also had warnings for the people about the consequences of their sinfulness, especially the sin of idolatry.

In chapter 51, Isaiah has some words of encouragement for those who want to obey God. '**Do not fear** the reproach of men, nor be afraid of their insults.' It is never easy to do right when all around you are people living carelessly, going their own way. Isaiah speaks of the future of those who have harsh words for God's people. He reminds those who love and obey God, that their opponents will soon be destroyed. In contrast, God's righteousness and His salvation, will continue for ever.

The world has not changed in its attitude to those who love God. In some countries at the present time, Christians are mocked and efforts are made to stop them giving teaching from the Bible. In other countries, there is cruel persecution of Christians, with imprisonment or forced labour. Isaiah's words from God, bring encouragement not just to people of his day, but to God's people at all times. We are to remember that wicked men will be judged by God, but those who love God will spend eternity with Him, where there is no sin, suffering or death, but joy, beauty and holiness.

Read

Isaiah 51:4-16; Matthew 10:16-22;
John 15:18-21.

Questions

1. What is the contrast in Isaiah 51:8? (Read verses 7-8).

2. What should we remember? (Isaiah 51:1-13).

3. Why should Christians not expect to be always treated well? (John 15:18 and 20).

23 A Young Man is Called to a Difficult Task

(Jeremiah 1:8)

Jeremiah was a young man when God told him that He had chosen him to be a prophet. Jeremiah knew that the work of a prophet was to hear God's message and tell others what God had said. He knew that this would not be easy, and he not only felt that he would not be able to speak to others, but he told God so.

God spoke to reassure Jeremiah, '… whatever I command you, you shall speak. **Do not be afraid** of their faces, for I am with you to deliver you.'

The people of Judah had turned away from the true God to worship idols. Jeremiah was called by God to be a prophet during the reign of King Josiah, Jehoiakim and Zedekiah. Josiah's father and especially his grandfather, King Manasseh, had encouraged the people in idolatry and all the evil things this led to. But in Josiah's time, a copy of God's law was found and read to the king. He began to do all he could to bring the people back to the true God. But after Josiah's reign, things in the nation only got worse. Jeremiah prophesied for forty years, warning the people of what would happen if they did not repent. He told them that the Babylonians would take them away from their land, because of their idolatry. The people would not listen. They hated Jeremiah and the message he gave them. They preferred their false prophets, who told them that all would be well.

Jeremiah suffered greatly. He was imprisoned and treated cruelly. But he also suffered because he loved his people, and could see them bringing God's punishment on themselves, because they refused to hear the warnings God sent by Jeremiah.

Jeremiah's life was hard, but he had God's promise to be with him, and he was faithful in carrying out the task God had given him.

Read

Jeremiah 1:1-10; 2:4-13; Lamentations 1:1-7.

Questions

1. What was the message that Jeremiah had to give to the people of Israel? (Jeremiah 2:9-13).

2. How did Jeremiah react when his warnings were ignored, and the people of Judah suffered because of their sin? (Lamentations 1:12).

24 Worthless and Useless Idols
(Jeremiah 10:5)

Israel was surrounded by nations who worshipped idols. They were false gods made out of wood or stone, gold or silver. They were unable to actually do anything, either good or evil. But they could be seen. Israel's God could not be seen.

No doubt the Israelites were well aware of the ceremonies, the offerings and the sacrifices which were a part of idolatry. It may have all seemed very impressive. But Jeremiah brought a message from God about idols. '**Do not be afraid** of them, for they cannot do evil, nor can they do any good.'

It may be that the Israelites were conscious that others looked down on them because they worshipped an unseen God. But Jeremiah contrasted the man-made idols, who could do nothing, with the greatness of God who created the earth. Why should anyone fear an idol made by a craftsman, however impressive it was made to look?

There are still false religions in the world. People still pray to their idols when they need help. Their prayers are not answered and no help comes. How we need to pray that God will help such men and women to turn to Him, the only true and living God.

Amy Carmichael was a missionary in India for many years. She saw elaborate processions as a particular idol was carried around. It all looked impressive. But she knew that there was no hope for those who trusted in their idols. She gave her whole life to bringing the good news, the gospel, for men and women and boys and girls.

Read

Jeremiah 10:1-16; Psalm 115:1-8.

Questions

1. How does Jeremiah describe idols?
   (Jeremiah 10:3-5 and 8-9).

2. How does he describe the true God?
   (Jeremiah 10:6-7 and 10-13).

3. An idol is anything put in the place of God. What sort of things can become idols in our own lives?

25 Fear of Living Under a Foreign Ruler

(Jeremiah 40:9)

God had given the people of Israel their own land and He promised to bless them in it, if they lived in obedience to Him. God had given His law to Israel, and His law was good because He knew what was best for them. The Ten Commandments in Exodus chapter 20 are there to protect life, to protect marriage, to protect property and to lead to truthfulness and contentment. But the first four commandments are about our duty to God. When those commandments are ignored, the others are soon broken.

The people of Judah had broken the first and second commandments by turning to idolatry. This was followed by treating others unjustly, not caring for the poor and many other wrongdoings. Over many years Jeremiah had given warnings from God that the people ignored. At last, all that Jeremiah had said was shown to be true. God would not allow His people to go on living in the land that He had given them. The Babylonian army carried many people away to Babylon as captives. But some of the poor people were left in Judah to take care of the land. Nebuchadnezzar, the king of Babylon, appointed a man named Gedaliah to be their governor.

Gedaliah gave wise advice to the people. '**Do not be afraid** to serve the Chaldeans. Dwell in the land and serve the King of Babylon, and it shall be well with you.' It is not pleasant to have a foreign ruler in charge of everything you do. But Gedaliah's advice was good because the people could not change their situation. It had happened because of their sin, and they must accept what God had caused to happen to them.

Read

Jeremiah 40:5-12; 2 Chronicles 36:11-21.

Questions

1. Why did God send messengers (the prophets) to His people with warnings of what would happen to them? (2 Chronicle 36:15).

2. Find the words in 2 Chronicles 36:16 that describe the people's reaction to God's messengers.

3. Poor people were left to live in the land of Judah (Jeremiah 39:10). What happened to others? (2 Chronicles 36:17 and 20).

26 Fear of Those the Prophet Must Speak to
(Ezekiel 2:6)

God had chosen Israel to be His own special people and an example to other nations. But they were constantly forgetting God's goodness to them, and wanting to be like the nations around them, with their idolatry. Those men who were chosen by God to be prophets, had a difficult task. When God called Ezekiel to be a prophet, He told him that he must give His messages to the people, but that they would not listen to him.

Ezekiel was among the captives taken to Babylon, and it was to those in captivity that he was to speak. God gave Ezekiel words of encouragement, along with a warning of the difficulty he would face. '… **do not be afraid** of them nor be afraid of their words … **do not be afraid** of their words or dismayed by their looks, though they are a rebellious house.'

God said that Ezekiel would be a 'watchman' to Israel. A watchman was someone who gave a warning when some danger was approaching. So Ezekiel was to warn the people of the consequences of their evil ways. This would give them the opportunity to repent: to stop their sinful actions. If he failed to warn the people, Ezekiel would be guilty. If his hearers refused to repent even after he had warned them, Ezekiel would be free from any guilt: he had given them a clear warning.

Ezekiel was obedient to God in speaking to the people. He was also given messages for other nations and visions that are recorded in the Book of Ezekiel.

Read

Ezekiel chapter 2, and chapter 33:1-11.

Questions

1. What was a watchman expected to do? (Ezekiel 33:1-6).

2. What was Ezekiel's responsibility as a watchman to Israel? (Ezekiel 33:7-9).

3. Does God want to punish people for their sinful ways? What does He ask them to do? (Ezekiel 33:11).

27 Fear in the Temple
(Luke 1:13)

Zacharias was a priest who carried out duties in the temple, as all the priests did. He was married to Elizabeth. They had prayed for a child, but as they grew older, it seemed that God had not granted their request.

In the temple there was an altar where incense was burned every morning and every evening. One day Zacharias was responsible for doing this, while the people gathered in the temple court for prayer. As he carried out his work, an angel appeared and said, '**Do not be afraid**, Zacharias, for your prayer is heard; and your wife Elizabeth will bear you a son, and you shall call his name John.' The angel went on to tell Zacharias that the birth of this child would be a time of rejoicing. Also, John would have a special work to do, preparing the people for the coming Saviour.

Zacharias found it hard to believe the angel's message. He and Elizabeth were older than people usually are when they become parents. The angel told him that because he had not believed God, he would be unable to speak until the baby was born.

The people waited for Zacharias and wondered why he had stayed so long in the temple. When he did come out, he could not speak to them, and they understood that he had seen a vision.

We can understand Zacharias' fear at the sight of an angel. The angel's words were reassuring: there was no need to fear, God was answering Zacharias and his wife's prayers in a wonderful way. The Old Testament contained prophecies of someone who would prepare the people for the coming of the Saviour. Zacharias and Elizabeth had been chosen by God to be the parents of a very special child.

Read

Luke 1:5-22; John 1:19-23; Isaiah 40:3.

Questions

1. When did God choose John for a special work? (Luke 1:13-15).

2. What effect would John have on the people? (Luke 1:16).

3. What did John understand about his work? (John 1:22-23 and Isaiah 40:3) *(The prophet Isaiah lived about 700 years before Jesus was born in Bethlehem.)*

28 An Unexpected Visitor
(Luke 1:30)

God sent the angel Gabriel with a message for a young woman named Mary. Mary lived in Nazareth and she was engaged to be married. The angel told Mary to rejoice because God had favoured her. Mary was troubled and did not understand the angel's words. The angel said, '**Do not be afraid**, Mary, for you have found favour with God.'

The angel then went on to explain that Mary would have a Son whose name would be Jesus. He would be the Son of God and Israel's true King. Again, Mary could not understand the angel's words. How could she, a young unmarried woman, have a child? Once again the angel explained. This birth would come about by the power of the Holy Spirit. The child to be born, would not have a human father.

We cannot understand how the Son of God, who had always been with His Father in heaven, could become a baby needing a mother to care for Him. But this is the way God chose, to send His Son into the world. God did not send the angel to a palace, to someone very wealthy or famous. He chose a young woman in an ordinary home, in a town in Galilee (the northern part of Israel).

We notice that the angel addressed Mary by name, which reminds us that God knows each one of us individually. God knew that Mary would carry out the task He had given her. She was not proud: she describes herself as 'lowly' (Luke 1:48). Mary had no need to fear the angel, who came to her with good news. Mary would never have wanted to be spoken of as a very special person, as some people speak of her. But she is an example to us of someone accepting with humility the message God had sent and the task He had chosen for her.

Read

Luke 1:26-38 and Luke 1:46-55; Isaiah 7:14.

Questions

1. How did Mary respond when she first saw the angel? (Luke 1:29).

2. What was Mary's very practical response to the angel's message? (Luke 1:34).

3. How would you describe Mary's final words to the angel? (Luke 1:38).

29 Fear of Making a Wrong Decision
(Matthew 1:20)

Joseph was a man who wanted to do the right thing. He was engaged to Mary and at that time a promise of marriage was taken very seriously and would not normally be broken. But Joseph had a problem. He knew that Mary was going to have a baby, so it seemed she must have acted wrongly and been unfaithful to her promise to him. He felt that he did not want her to be disgraced in other people's eyes. He thought he must end their engagement with as little fuss as possible.

While Joseph was still thinking about how he should deal with the situation, an angel appeared to him in a dream. The angel brought a message from God: some amazing news and some words of reassurance. 'Joseph … **do not be afraid** to take to you Mary your wife, for that which is conceived in her is of the Holy Spirit.' The angel then told Joseph that the baby must be given the name Jesus (a name that means Saviour).

Joseph believed the angel's message and looked after Mary and her child. He would probably have known that the prophet Isaiah had foretold this special birth (Isaiah 7:14). He understood that Mary had not been unfaithful to him because this child had no human father. This was a miraculous birth: Jesus was the Son of God, who came to 'save His people from their sins' (Matthew 1:21).

No doubt Mary and Joseph believed all that was written in the Old Testament about the Saviour who God had promised to send. They were chosen by God to care for His Son during His early years. They were obedient to all God's messages to them and faithfully carried out the responsibility He had given them.

Read

Matthew 1:18-25; Isaiah 7:14.

Questions

1. Why did the angel call Joseph 'son of David'? (Matthew 1:1, 6 and 16).

2. How do we know that Joseph believed the angel's message? (Matthew 1:24).

3. What names does the prophet Isaiah give to the promised Saviour? (Isaiah 7:14 and 9:6).

30 The Shepherds' Fear
(Luke 2:10)

Before the promised baby was born, Mary and Joseph had to go from Nazareth to Bethlehem. The Roman emperor, Caesar Augustus, had said that everyone must go to the place their family first came from, to be registered. Mary and Joseph were descendants of King David whose hometown was Bethlehem. It was a journey of about eighty-five miles, not easy when there were no cars, trains or aeroplanes.

It was while they were in Bethlehem that Jesus was born. There was no crib with cosy blankets for the baby, but He was laid in a manger, which would normally have held the animals' food.

Out in the field near Bethlehem, some shepherds were looking after their sheep. It was night-time, but the shepherds were startled by a brightness. They saw an angel standing near them and they were very frightened. The first words that the angel spoke were, **'Do not be afraid.'** The angel told the shepherds that he brought good news. God's promised Saviour had been born in Bethlehem and they would find Him lying in a manger. Many angels then appeared, praising God.

The shepherds wasted no time in going to Bethlehem and they found the baby just as the angel had told them. After they had seen the Lord Jesus, the shepherds told others all that the angel had told them about the baby.

The birth of God's own Son, the Lord Jesus, was so special that God sent angels to take His messages. The Bible tells us that angels protect those who trust in the Lord Jesus, but they are usually unseen. The sudden appearance of an angel caused fear, but the angel spoke words of reassurance so that those they spoke to could hear their message without being afraid.

Read

Luke 2:1–20; Micah 5:2 (The prophet Micah wrote about Bethlehem being the place where the promised Saviour would be born, about 700 years before.)

Questions

1. Who did the angel bring good news for? (Luke 2:10).

2. What did the angel call Bethlehem? (Luke 2:11).

3. What were the many angels who appeared, doing? (Luke 2:13).

31 A Miracle that Caused Fear
(Luke 5:10)

Simon Peter and his brother Andrew were fishermen. They worked with two other brothers, James and John, at the Sea of Galilee. One night they had fished all night long and had not caught any fish. The next day, as they were washing their nets, the Lord Jesus came and stood on the shore. A great crowd had gathered and so Jesus asked Simon Peter to move his boat a little way from the land. Jesus was able to speak to the crowd from the boat.

When He had finished speaking, Jesus asked Simon Peter to launch his boat and let the net down ready for a catch. Simon Peter explained that they had worked all night without catching anything, but he did as Jesus had told him. So many fish filled the net that Peter and Andrew had to signal to James and John to come and help them. The fish they had caught, filled both boats. The number of fish was unusually large: even causing those four experienced fishermen to be astonished. Peter bowed down before the Lord Jesus, saying, 'Depart from me, for I am a sinful man, O Lord!' Jesus replied, '**Do not be afraid**. From now on you will catch men.'

Peter had realised that he was in the presence of Someone who was no ordinary man. He felt his own sinfulness and that he was not worthy to be with Jesus. But encouraged by Jesus' words, all four fishermen became disciples: followers of Jesus who would learn from Him and then be able to teach others. Jesus' words about 'catching men' meant that they would lead people to trust in Him. After the Lord Jesus had returned to heaven, we read of three thousand people becoming Christians, when Peter spoke to them (Acts 2:41).

Read

Luke 5:1-11 *(Lake Gennesaret is another name for the Sea of Galilee.)*

Questions

1. How do we know that this catch was quite different from the number of fish the men usually caught? (verse 9).

2. Why did Peter feel afraid? (verse 8).

3. How did the lives of the four fishermen change? (verse 11).

32 A Father's Fear
(Mark 5:36)

Jairus was a leader in the synagogue. Many cities in Israel had one or more synagogues. (These were buildings where the Jewish people met, to be taught from the Old Testament, and to worship God.) One day Jairus came to Jesus in great distress. His only daughter, who was twelve years old, was very, very ill. He bowed down before Jesus and begged Him to come and heal his daughter.

Jesus went with Jairus, but before they reached his house, there was someone else who needed healing. A woman who had been ill for twelve years, believed that if she came quietly behind Jesus and just touched His clothing, she would be made well. This did happen, but the Lord Jesus knew what had happened and He spoke to her. It must have been hard for Jairus to wait, fearing that his daughter might die. Just at that time someone came from his house to tell him that she had died and so there was no need for Jesus to come.

Hearing what had been said, Jesus spoke to Jairus: '**Do not be afraid**; only believe.' People had gathered at Jairus' house to mourn for the child and they were weeping loudly. Jesus put them outside, only allowing Jairus and his wife with Peter, James and John to go into the room where the child lay. At His words, 'Little girl, I say to you, arise', she did just that. Jairus' sadness was turned to joy: his daughter was given back to him.

The Lord Jesus had shown His power to give life to one who had been dead. The Bible tells us that we are all dead towards God because of our sin. The Lord Jesus gives new life to all who trust Him for forgiveness. When our sin has been forgiven, we can know God as our greatest Friend.

Read

Mark 5:21-43; 2 Corinthians 5:17; Ephesians 2:1.

Questions

1. Which verses in Mark chapter 5 show that Jesus had power over disease?

2. Which verses show that He had power over death?

3. How is the change that happens when someone becomes a Christian described in 2 Corinthians 5:17? How is it described in Ephesians 2:1?

33 When the Disciples were Afraid
(Matthew 14:27)

It had been an extraordinary day. King Herod had had John the Baptist put to death. Then the Lord Jesus had gone to a quiet place, but great crowds had followed Him there, and Jesus healed those who were ill. In the evening, the disciples asked Jesus to send the people away so that they could buy food. Jesus replied that there was no need for the people to go.

The Lord Jesus took control of the situation. He asked the disciples to make the people sit down on the grass, in groups of fifty. He took five loaves and two fish and began handing them to the disciples. There was enough food for all and twelve baskets full of leftover pieces. Over five thousand people had eaten enough to satisfy them.

While Jesus sent the crowds away, He asked the disciples to get into their boat and cross to the other side of the lake. He then spent some time alone in prayer to His Father in heaven.

The disciples did not have an easy crossing. The wind was against them and they were tossed about by the waves. The Lord Jesus began walking towards them on the sea. The disciples were afraid, thinking they were seeing a ghost. Jesus said, 'Be of good cheer! It is I; **do not be afraid.'**

Peter wanted to meet the Lord Jesus on the water. So Jesus told him to come. Peter began to walk towards Jesus, but when he saw how stormy it was, he became afraid and began to sink. When he cried out for help, Jesus caught hold of him and they got into the boat.

This true story has something to teach us. We sometimes come into frightening situations. When we concentrate on the situation, we become fearful like Peter did. But when we remember Jesus' promise never to leave us, our fears are calmed.

Read

Matthew 14:1-33; Mark 6:31-51.

Questions

1. The Lord Jesus had gone to a quiet place. What was His attitude to the crowds who followed Him there? (Matthew 14:14).

2. What was His response when the disciples wanted to send the people away? (Matthew 14:16).

3. What was Jesus' response to Peter? (Matthew 14:28-29 and 30-31).

34 Fear on the Mountain
(Matthew 17:7)

One day, the Lord Jesus took three of His disciples, Peter, James and John, up onto a high mountain. The three disciples had no idea that they were going to see something very wonderful that day. As Jesus was praying, a great change happened. There was a brightness in His face like the shining of the sun. His clothes became white like light itself. But there was something else. Two men were with Him who had not come up the mountain with Jesus. They knew that one man was Moses and the other was Elijah.

Jesus was talking with Moses and Elijah. They were speaking about all that was going to happen in Jerusalem where Jesus would die on the cross. The disciples did not know what to do or say. Peter said he would make three tabernacles (tents), one for each of them. At that moment they were overshadowed by a cloud and they heard a voice saying, 'This is my beloved Son, in whom I am well pleased. Hear Him!'

Hearing that voice, the disciples fell down in fear. The Lord Jesus touched them and said, 'Arise, and **do not be afraid**.' When they looked up, only Jesus was with them. As they came down from the mountain, He told them not to tell anyone what they had seen, until He had risen from the dead. They did not understand what He meant by rising from the dead, but they were careful not to tell anyone what they had seen. Peter did write about it years later (2 Peter 1:17-18). We can be quite sure that those three disciples never forgot what they had seen that day.

God is very great and He is holy. We are sinful people and so it is not surprising that the voice of God from heaven caused the disciples to be afraid. We can come to God without fear, only when we know that our sin is forgiven because we trust in the Lord Jesus.

Read

Matthew 17:1-9; Luke 9:28-36; 2 Peter 1:17-18.

Questions

1. Moses gave God's _ _ _ to the people (John 1:17).

2. Elijah was a _ _ _ _ _ _ _ _ (1 Kings 18:36).

3. What did Moses and Elijah speak about? (Luke 9:31).

75

35 Words to Take Away Fear
(John 14:27)

It was a strange and a sad time for the disciples. They had followed the Lord Jesus, believing that He was the Saviour God had promised to send. But they had not understood when He had spoken to them about His death and His resurrection. Now, while they were together, sharing the Passover meal, Jesus spoke to them about going away, somewhere that they could not follow Him. They still did not understand.

More words caused them to be perplexed as well as sad. Jesus said, 'One of you will betray Me.' How could it be possible that one of His twelve closest friends would betray Him to His enemies? Then when Peter bravely said that he would lay down his life for Jesus, the Lord told him that before the morning dawned, he would not just once, but three times deny that he ever knew Jesus.

The Lord Jesus knew all that would soon happen to Him. This was the last time He would talk to His disciples before His crucifixion. He told them that the Holy Spirit would come to them and would help them. His thoughts were for these men who had been with

Him. He spoke words of comfort, 'Let not your heart be troubled, neither let it be afraid.'

Jesus knew that His disciples needed these words. Much was about to happen that could cause great fear. When Jesus was arrested, put on trial, cruelly treated and then crucified, what would happen to the disciples? Would the enemies of Jesus come looking for them also?

In John's gospel chapters 14–16 we read how Jesus spoke to His disciples at this time. We cannot fail to notice His care and thoughtfulness for them. What an encouragement to all who trust in the Lord Jesus, that He has such great love for all who follow Him.

Read

John 13:21-38 and chapter 14.

Questions

1. What two things did Jesus know about the disciples? (John 13:21 and 38).

2. Why could the disciples become afraid at this time? (John 13:33).

3. What is the proof that we love the Lord Jesus? (John 14:15).

36 Resurrection Day: The Angel's Words
(Matthew 28: 5-7)

The disciples and the women who had been helpers to the Lord Jesus, had spent a very sad Sabbath day, after the crucifixion. Then, very early in the morning, on the first day of the week, some of the women set off for the place where the body of Jesus had been placed. The tomb was a cave with a heavy stone across the entrance. The women wondered how they could move the stone, but when they came to the place, they found the stone had already been moved.

It was an angel who had moved the stone. The men who had been ordered to guard the tomb, in case the disciples stole the body of Jesus, trembled at the sight of the angel. But when the angel spoke to the women, he said, '**Do not be afraid** …' The angel explained that the body was not there, because the Lord Jesus had risen from the dead. The women were told to go and tell the disciples that Jesus had risen, and that they would see Him in Galilee. The Bible describes death as the last enemy (1 Corinthians 15:26) and it is the result of the entry of sin into the world (Genesis 2:17

and Romans 6:23). How amazed the women must have been, to find that Jesus had conquered death. All the sadness they had felt since the crucifixion was gone. Now they knew without a doubt, that Jesus is the Son of God.

The disciples had not understood when Jesus had spoken to them of His death and resurrection. They would still find it hard to believe, until they actually saw Him. In future, their task would be to tell others about the Saviour who had conquered sin and death for all who trust in Him.

Read

Mathew chapter 28; Isaiah chapter 53.

Questions

1. Can you find a promise of resurrection in Isaiah 53:10-12?

2. What practical matter troubled the women as they set off for the tomb? (Mark 16:3).

3. How many times in Matthew 28 were the women told not to be afraid? Who said this to them?

37 Paul is Encouraged
(Acts 18:9)

In the course of his missionary travels, the apostle Paul came to the Greek city of Corinth. This was the Roman capital of the region known as Achaia, and Paul spent eighteen months there. Corinth was known for its luxurious, but sinful, lifestyle. At the beginning of his time in the city, Paul spent every Sabbath day speaking in the synagogue. But the Jews there would not accept that Jesus was the Christ: the One God had promised to send. Paul then concentrated on the Gentiles, the non-Jewish people, although Crispus, the ruler of the synagogue, did believe in the Lord Jesus Christ.

One night, God spoke to Paul in a vision. God said, '**Do not be afraid**, but speak, and do not keep silent … for I have many people in this city.' How encouraging these words must have been to the apostle. Everywhere he went, while some people believed the message he brought, he often met with opposition. But God knew the people of that city and He knew that many would become Christians.

Some of the Jews at Corinth were so angry because of Paul's message, that they tried to make a case against him. But the local official, a man named Gallio, would have nothing to do with the matter. God had spoken truly that no-one would be able to harm Paul in that city. He had known ill-treatment and imprisonment in other places, but for eighteen months he was able to teach at Corinth. What a great joy for him, when many believed the gospel and were baptized.

Read

Acts 18:1-16.

Questions

1. How did Paul support himself in his travels and who was he able to work with at Corinth? (verses 1-3).

2. Find four encouragements in God's words to Paul (verses 9-10).

3. There were some discouragements for Paul at Corinth especially among the Jewish people. But what surprising conversions were there? (verse 8).

38 An Angel's Words in the Storm
(Acts 27:23-24)

The apostle Paul was on his way to Rome by sea. He was a prisoner, although the charges against him were false. He was put on board a ship with other prisoners. But Paul knew that sailing late in the year could be dangerous. He was proved right when a very severe storm occurred. The sailors did everything they knew in such a situation, including lightening the ship by throwing everything they could overboard.

The sailors gave up hope of ever reaching land, but Paul stood and spoke to them all. He told them about an angel who had appeared to him during the night. The angel had said, '**Do not be afraid**, Paul …' and went on to tell him that he would certainly be brought before Caesar and that God would bring everyone on board safely to land. Paul then told the sailors that he believed God. He encouraged them to have some food, because they had been fasting for two weeks. The men listened to Paul and were so encouraged by his words that they did take some food.

There were 276 people on the ship Paul travelled on. How was it that Paul the prisoner was able to influence and encourage others as he did? How was it that he was calm even when experienced seamen were afraid? The answer is that Paul believed God: he knew that God always does what He promises to do. The Bible contains many promises that are given to everyone who trusts in the Lord Jesus. What a difference it makes to our lives, when we know that He will never leave us (Matthew 28:20) and that there is nothing that can ever separate us from His love (Romans 8:38-39). As you read your Bible each day, memorise some of the promises you find there.

Read

Acts chapter 27.

Questions

1. What two things did Paul do with the message the angel brought? (verses 23-25).

2. Did Paul keep his love for God to himself? (verse 35).

3. What was the practical way in which God's promise was fulfilled? (verses 42-44).

39 Words of Encouragement to Christians
(1 Peter 3:14)

Peter had been a disciple of the Lord Jesus, hearing Him speak and seeing the wonderful things that He did. He had also seen and spoken with Jesus after His resurrection. So Peter became an apostle: sent by the Lord Jesus to be His witness to others who needed to hear of Him. Two letters written by Peter are recorded in the New Testament. He wrote his first letter to help Christians who were scattered throughout the lands of the Middle East.

Peter gives some practical advice for living as a Christian. He has some words for servants and for husbands and wives. Then he writes about how Christians may suffer, not because they have done wrong, but simply because they are living out their faith. In 1 Peter 3:14 he quotes from the prophet Isaiah, 'And **do not be afraid** of their threats, nor be troubled' (Isaiah 8:12). He gives the great example of how Christ suffered, not for His own sins but for the sins of others. He had already written about this in his words to those who were servants of masters who could treat them harshly (1 Peter 2:20-23).

It has been true through the centuries that Christians have suffered because of their faith. At the present time, Christians in many countries are being persecuted: harshly treated or even killed. Even in the West, Christians who obey the Bible's teaching, can find themselves in trouble. It is good to remember the words of Isaiah quoted by Peter. We are not to be afraid or troubled. We remember the warning that Jesus gave to His followers, that those who hated Him will also hate them (John 15:18). We are to look forward to the time when the Lord Jesus will come again, and we shall be with Him.

Read

Isaiah 8:12; 1 Peter 2:18-25 and 1 Peter 3:8-18.

Questions

1. In what way is the Lord Jesus an example to those who suffer harsh treatment, when they have done no wrong? (1 Peter 2:21-23).

2. How should Christians react to unkind words? (1 Peter 3:9).

3. Which words in 1 Peter 2:20, describe how Christians should act when they are wronged?

40 When the Apostle John was Afraid
(Revelation 1:17)

John was one of Jesus' twelve disciples. He had been with Jesus for about three years and had even talked with Him during the last meal Jesus shared before His crucifixion. He wrote one of the four gospels and three letters that are included in the new Testament.

John was living on the Island of Patmos, in the Aegean Sea, south of Samos. He was there as an exile, because of his Christian life and the teaching he gave. While he was there, he was given wonderful visions of heaven and of things that were to happen before the return of the Lord Jesus Christ. He was also given messages to teach the church at all times.

When John saw the Lord Jesus, he fell down before Him as if he was dead. But Jesus spoke words of comfort, '**Do not be afraid** … I am He who lives, and was dead, and behold, I am alive for evermore …' John was seeing the Lord Jesus in all His glory, and the sight was almost too much for him. This reminds us of how the Lord humbled Himself when He came into the world and lived as a man. John had known Him then, but seeing Him in the glory of heaven almost overwhelmed him.

John was instructed to write all he saw and heard in the visions he was given. This is what we have as the Book of the Revelation. The Roman authorities may have thought they could silence the apostle John, by sending him into exile, but millions of people must have read the words he wrote in this book.

If we have trusted in the Lord Jesus to forgive our sins, we can know Him as our greatest Friend. But we always have reverence (great respect) for Him, because He is above us in His holiness and His great power and wisdom.

Read

Revelation chapter 1.

Questions

1. What was John's occupation when Jesus called him to follow Him? (Matthew 4:18-22).

2. How does John refer to himself in the Gospel he wrote? (John 19:26; 20:2; 21:20).

3. Where does John see the Lord Jesus standing and what does this mean? (Revelation 1:13 and 20).

Good Choices, Bad Choices
by Jean Stapleton

The Bible teaches us that God always does what He says He will do. It is a great comfort to know, that God's plans and purposes are not changed by men and women who make wrong or foolish choices. In a way that we cannot understand, God rules over everything, so that His promises are always fulfilled. From the first wrong choice made by Adam and Eve throughout the Bible we meet many people who chose well or who made foolish decisions. This book will help you to focus on God's Word and his wisdom guiding you in your own day to day choices.

ISBN: 978-1-5271-0527-0

More Good Choices, Bad Choices
by Jean Stapleton

The Bible teaches us that God always does what He says He will do. It is a great comfort to know, that God's plans and purposes are not changed by men and women who make wrong or foolish choices. In a way that we cannot understand, God rules over everything, so that His promises are always fulfilled. Young and old, rich and poor all appear in the Bible and through them we see examples of people who made wise and foolish decisions. This book will help you to focus on God's Word and his wisdom guiding you in your own day to day choices.

ISBN: 978-1-5271-0528-7

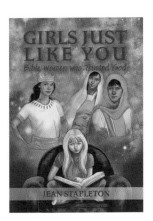

Girls Just Like You
by Jean Stapleton

We might think that people in Bible times were different from us (much braver and better than we are), but that isn't true. They were just like us – just like you, in fact! There are fifty different stories in this book, with Bible verses to read that will teach you about the girls and women in the Bible who trusted God. Find out about them and about yourself by discovering God's Word that He has written for you!

ISBN: 978-1-78191-997-2

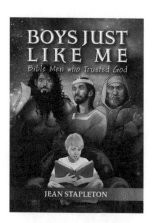

Boys Just Like Me
by Jean Stapleton

We might think that people in Bible times were different from us (much braver and better than we are), but that isn't true. They were just like us – just like you, in fact! There are fifty different stories in this book, with Bible verses to read that will teach you about the boys and men in the Bible who trusted God. Find out about them and about yourself by discovering God's Word that He has written for you!

ISBN: 978-1-78191-998-9

God's Special Tent
by Jean Stapleton

Do you like tents? Perhaps you've gone camping, staying in one place and then moving to another. God's people the Israelites lived in tents in the wilderness as they moved from Egypt to the Promised Land. God gave them instructions about how to make a special tent - where He could be present among His people. The priests made sacrifices to atone for the sin of the people, but the tabernacle or tent of meeting was a place that taught the people about the one who was going to save them from their sin for good – Jesus Christ, the promised Messiah. His sacrifice would mean that no other sacrifices were needed and that people could worship God all around the world.

ISBN: 978-1-84550-811-1

Read with me
by Jean Stapleton

Read with Me takes the stories and teachings of the Bible from the beginning of the Old Testament through to the end of the New, explaining them in simple, direct language. These devotions are ideal for reading to children – each one bringing out truths and questions, answers and lessons – and will bring your family closer to God.

For older family members there is also an additional feature where, throughout the book, introductions are given to those Old and New Testament books that are featured. These give useful information for older children – or for adults to read alongside the family devotions.

ISBN: 978-1-84550-148-8

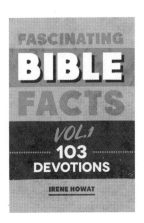

Fascinating Bible Facts Vol. 1
by Irene Howat

There are some surprising stories in God's Word about
animals, trees and forests, and families – amongst other
things. In Fascinating Bible Facts Vol. 1, you will find out
about the beginning of time, but also discover the most
amazing place that ever was or will be – heaven!

Each of the devotions has a Bible Promise for you to read.
Throughout the book, find out the questions Chloe has
for you to answer, the facts that Abbi has for you to learn,
and the activities that Zac has for you to do.

ISBN: 978-1-5271-0143-2

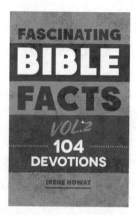

Fascinating Bible Facts Vol. 2
by Irene Howat

How about going on a fact–finding expedition? This journey will take you into the past and the future by introducing you to the magnificent, amazing, fascinating Bible!

Each of the devotions has a Bible Promise for you to read. Throughout the book, find out the questions Chloe has for you to answer, the facts that Abbi has for you to learn, and the activities that Zac has for you to do.

ISBN: 978-1-5271-0144-9

CHRISTIAN FOCUS PUBLICATIONS

Christian   Christian   CF4K   Mentor
Focus   Heritage

Christian Focus Publications publishes books for adults
and children under its four main imprints: Christian Focus,
CF4K, Mentor and Christian Heritage. Our books reflect
our conviction that God's Word is reliable and Jesus is the
way to know him, and live for ever with him.

Our children's publication list covers pre-school to early
teens. We also publish personal and family devotional
titles, biographies and inspirational stories that
children will love.

From pre-school board books to teenage apologetics, we
have it covered!

Christian Focus Publications Ltd,
Geanies House, Fearn, Ross-shire,
IV20 1TW, Scotland,
United Kingdom.
www.christianfocus.com

CF4•K
Because you're never
too young to know Jesus